US ARMY ATTACK HELICOPTER UNIT PATCHES (2001-20

CW4 DAN McCLINTON (USA/RET)

M000276786

INTRODUCTION

Welcome to this second in a series of books featuring the patches and insignia of aviation units of the United States Army. As you may have deduced by the title this volume will feature the insignia used by Attack Helicopter Units during the time period of September 11, 2001 until the year 2020.

For those that are unfamiliar with the structure and organization of modern Army Aviation a quick history lesson might be in order. The birth of modern Army Aviation occurred during the Vietnam War when helicopters began to be used in battle in large numbers. During that conflict the first purpose-built Attack Helicopter (AH-1 Cobra) saw service in Air Cavalry Troops and Aerial Rocket Artillery units. When the Vietnam War ended and the focus was changed towards the Cold War and possible conflict with the Soviet Union the use of the armed helicopter as a anti-armor weapon was begun. With that came the formation of Attack Helicopter Battalions and the development of what was to become the AH-64 Apache attack helicopter.

On September 11, 2001 the United States Army was in a state of transition to what at that time was called "digital warfighting". A major part of that transition was the replacement of the existing AH-64A airframes with AH-64D Longbow Apaches. Additionally, during that time period divisions that were designated "light" (10th Mountain, 25th Infantry and the 82nd Airborne) were equipped with the OH-58D aircraft in their Attack Helicopter Battalions. This largely remained true until around 2005-2007 when the Army began a reorganization process where all Attack Helicopter Battalions were equipped with the AH-64. This remains true until 2020 with the AH-64 fleet gradually converting to the AH-64E.

BLACK OVER WHITE: THE ATTACK COLORS

As you may have noticed many Attack patches feature the colors black and white. Much like the Cavalry uses red over white, attack helicopter units in the US Army use black over white. When this began or what it actually stands for has been lost or is a point of contention. Many say that the black over white started because many attack units were formed from former cavalry troops and squadrons and they wished to mimic their former units. By US Army regulation attack helicopter companies are issued the standard aviation blue guidon (as seen in the photo below), Many units however, self purchase black over white guidons and fly them proudly, often while deployed to combat (see below). As for the meaning behind the practice, it has been said that the black either stands for the hours of darkness or death with white alternately meaning daylight (24 hour operations) or surrender (meaning death before surrender). To the author the representation of 24 hour operations, especially with the introduction of the AH-64 helicopter makes more sense, but I am unable to find an official explanation either way.

A CO 1-82 AVN standard AVN Company Guidon
(Photo courtesy of Shon Thompson)

1-227 AVN BN Colors Camp Taji, Iraq 2004
(Author's photo)

TABLE OF CONTENTS

THE APACHE PATCH

Many of you may have noticed that most of the patches that have been or are being used for attack helicopter units that are equipped with versions of the AH-64 Apache have a definite theme. While there is no authority or regulation that governs the production, appearance or even wearing of company, troop, battalion or squadron level patches for US Army Aviation there is an undeniable feeling of tradition and a strong push to remember those who came before.

When the AH-64 was named after the Native American Apache tribe in 1981, the art department of the Hughes Helicopter Company also unveiled its logo for the new aircraft (see photo bottom left) and the rest was history. When the aircraft began to be delivered to line units in the mid 80's virtually all unit patches/insignia were based on the original Apache program patch. This tradition has continued (as one can plainly see by the patch designs displayed in this book) to this day. There is symbolism contained in many of these designs. If you look at the original Apache program patch there are 6 stars in the border of the patch, many say this is to recognize that the 6th Air Cavalry Brigade was the first unit to field the Apache. Interestingly enough the 6th US Cavalry was the unit that hunted down and captured the Apache Indian leader Geronimo during the Indian Wars of the mid to late 1800's. Other patch designs have featured 10 stars which represent the original 10 divisional attack battalions. As anyone familiar with US Army Aviation patches can readily attest there is often no rhyme or reason as to why patches contain the things that they do, or the reasons have been lost to history. In the case of this book, the patches are presented as is with little to no explanation other than unit identification.

Any errors you may find are totally the fault of the author and all credit goes to those that have gratefully given time and assets to make the volume of patches the best that it can possibly be. ENJOY!

4

2 AH-64D aircraft belonging to 1-227th AVN, 1 CD takeoff from Camp Taji, Iraq. (2007 photo by author)

SUPER PRIMUM

1-1 AVN Battalion Patches

| A Company 1-1 AVN "DEVILS" | | | | A CO 1-1 AVN "REBELS" |

| B Company 1-1 AVN "WOLFPACK" |

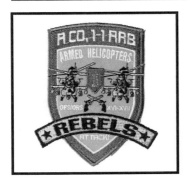    

| C Company 1-1 AVN "GHOSTRIDERS" |

INTERESTING FACT: *The gun platoon of A Company 1st Aviation Battalion, 1st Infantry Division in Vietnam was named the"Rebels". Their aircraft were also painted with associated "rebel" imagery. A Company 1-1 ARB renamed the company Rebels to honor the heritage of those that served before them in the 1st Infantry Division. Obviously, the controversy that surrounds the Confederate battle flag made an exact reproduction of the old unit patch undesirable. It is great to see units honor their history. This is a practice that is common in other services of the Armed Forces and it is showing up in the US Army with more regularity.*

1-2 AVN Battalion Patches

Gunfighters continued...   **A Company 1-2 AVN "RAZORBACKS"**

Razorbacks continued...   **B Company 1-2 AVN "PALADIN"**

  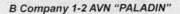   

D Company 1-2 AVN "ROADRUNNERS"

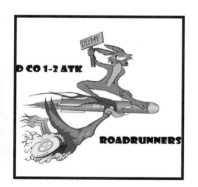

E Company 1-2 AVN "GLADIATORS"

4-2 AVN Battalion Patches

A Company 4-2 AVN "ARCHANGEL"

B Company 4-2 AVN "GRIM REAPERS"

D Company 4-2 AVN "HELLHOUNDS"

E Company 4-2 AVN "UNDERTAKERS"   HHC 4-2 AVN "HORSEMEN"

EX ALIS PUGNAMUS

1-3 AVN Battalion and Task Force Patches

A Company 1-3 AVN "ASSASSINS"

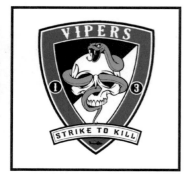    

B Cmpany 1-3 AVN "WARLORDS"

C Company 1-3 AVN "OUTCASTS"

HHC 1-3 AVN "COBRAS"

EX ALIS PUGNAMUS

3-3 AVN Battalion Patches

A Company 3-3 AVN "DEATH STALKERS" — B Company 3-3 AVN "KILLER SPADE"

C Company 3-3 AVN "BLUE MAX"

1-4 AVN Battalion and Task Force Patches

REAPERS cont...	C Company 1-4 AVN "SIDEWINDERS"

SIDEWINDERS cont...	D Company 1-4 AVN "DAWGS"

E Company 1-4 AVN "ROUGHRIDERS"	HHC 1-4 AVN

4th Battalion 4th Aviation Regiment "GAMBLER GUNS"

4th Infantry Division, Fort Hood, TX / Fort Carson. CO (AH-64D) OIF, OFS

4-4 AVN Battalion and Task Force Patches

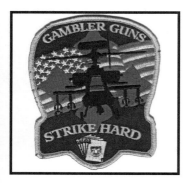

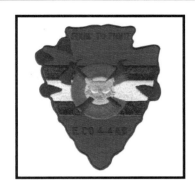

HHC 4-4 AVN "HIGH ROLLERS"

INTERESTING FACT *Both 1-4 and 4-4 Attack Reconnaissance Battalions (belonging to the 4th Infantry Division) moved around quite a bit during the Global War on Terror. 1-4 ATK was based at FT Hood, TX with its parent unit on 9/11, 4-4 ATK came into being later when heavy divisions removed aviation troops from the division cavalry squadrons. In the case of 4ID, 1st Squadron 10th Cavalry lost its OH-58D troops, which were replaced in the division by another attack helicopter battalion which had at that time been renamed Attack-Reconnaissance battalions. This was typical in the heavy divisions at that time, so units like 1st Armored Division, 1st Cavalry Division, 2nd Infantry Division, 3rd Infantry Division and the 4th Infantry Divisions all lost their division cavalry elements which were replaced by a second attack helicopter battalion. The 1st Infantry Division is also considered a heavy division, but due to its position in deployment rotation, it never received a second attack battalion.*

When 1-4 AVN was stationed at FT Hood, many of its patches featured items that identified its Texas home, when the unit moved to FT Carson, CO those elements were replaced in many cases by depictions of Colorado. An interesting by-product of the moving and shifting of units.

1-10 AVN Battalion and Task Force Patches

A Company 1-10 AVN "ROGUES"

A Company 1-10 AVN "DEATH STALKERS"

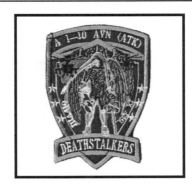

DEATH STALKERS continued....   **A CO 1-10 AVN "PITCH BLACK"**

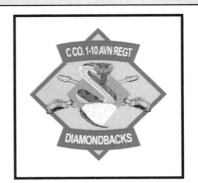

DIAMONDBACKS continued...   **C Company 1-10 AVN "BLUE MAX"**

BLUE MAX continnued...   **C Company 1-10 AVN "COBRAS"**

Graphic courtesy of 1-10 ARB, 10th Mountain Division, US Army

WHAT'S IN A NAME?
BLUE MAX: THE ISSUE OF UNIT NAME CHANGES AND WHY IT OCCURS

Over the years as the United States Army has expanded and then "down-sized" various units come and go. As a result often units with outstanding combat records find themselves being "re-flagged" as another unit that the Army has deemed to be more historically relevant with their former unit designation sent to the dustbin of history. The subsequent shifting and re-naming of assigned companies makes if difficult for a historian or patch collector to follow the legacy of a particular unit. This combined with the unofficial nature of assigning company names within the US Army only helps add to the confusion.

To help illustrate the confusion and hopefully explain how it occurs, I will use all units that have used the name "Blue Max" as an example. As with most things that pertain to US Army aviation, the story starts in Vietnam. During the Vietnam War the 1st Cavalry Division (Airmobile) had several aviation units assigned to it. Among those was the 2nd Battalion 20th Aerial Rocket Artillery (2-20 ARA) BLUE MAX.

After the end of hostilities in Vietnam, the Blue Max moniker appeared once again, this time under the flag of 1-229th AVN which was stationed at FT Bragg, NC at the time. Over the years the name has been used by 3-101, 3-3 AVN, 1-10 AVN and 1-229th again when it was reconstituted at FT Lewis, WA. The most direct lineage to the original Blue Max would be C CO 1-229th which as far as can be determined was the first unit after Vietnam to use that name.

It is understandable that soldiers assigned to units that undergo name changes want to bring the old names with them to the new unit, especially when the Army doesn't control the naming of company level organizations and unit patches are soldier resourced and controlled. It does however lead to unintended consequences. In the case of Blue Max, memorabilia that had been saved by soldiers since Vietnam was scattered around the Army ending up at FT Campbell, FT Lewis and FT Drum. This situation was resolved between unit commanders with the memorabilia ultimately making its way to the 1-229th at FT Lewis, WA, but since there is no system in place to track these things, the only thing that insured this happened was having people in place that actually cared about the history of the units involved.

Readers of this may conclude that I am advocating that the Army institute some control of patches and units names. This is certainly not the case as I firmly believe that if the Army took control of those things the practice of producing unit and morale patches would be so neutered and sanitized that it would ultimately kill it. I am only noting these things so those that are unfamiliar with Army practices can understand it better.

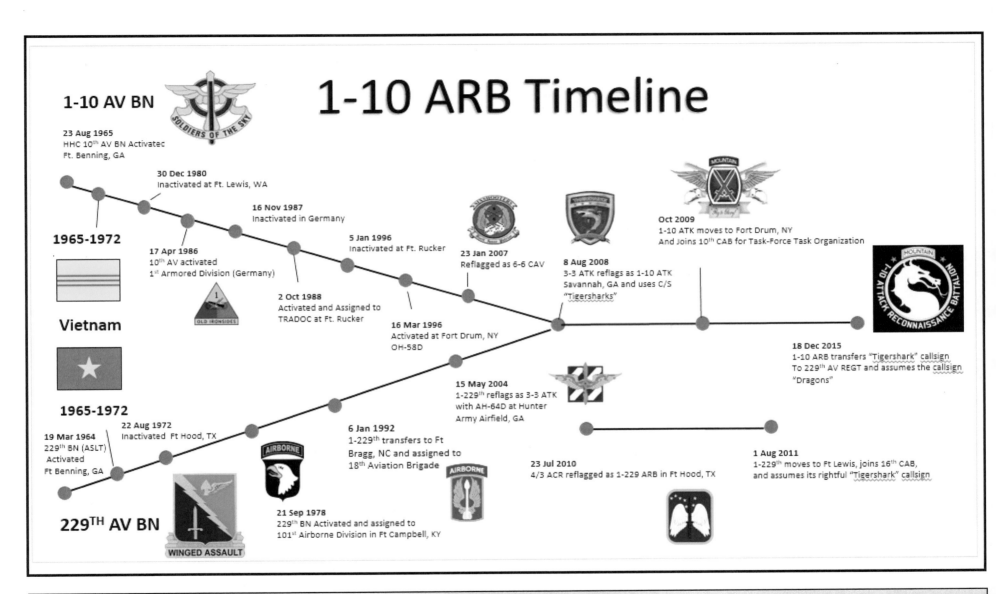

1-10 ARB Timeline

1-10 AV BN

23 Aug 1965
HHC 10th AV BN Activated
Ft. Benning, GA

30 Dec 1980
Inactivated at Ft. Lewis, WA

16 Nov 1987
Inactivated in Germany

1965-1972

5 Jan 1996
Inactivated at Ft. Rucker

17 Apr 1986
10th AV activated
1st Armored Division (Germany)

23 Jan 2007
Reflagged as 6-6 CAV

Oct 2009
1-10 ATK moves to Fort Drum, NY
And Joins 10th CAB for Task-Force Task Organization

Vietnam

2 Oct 1988
Activated and Assigned to
TRADOC at Ft. Rucker

8 Aug 2008
3-3 ATK reflags as 1-10 ATK
Savannah, GA and uses C/S
"Tigersharks"

16 Mar 1996
Activated at Fort Drum, NY
OH-58D

18 Dec 2015
1-10 ARB transfers "Tigershark" callsign
To 229th AV REGT and assumes the callsign
"Dragons"

1965-1972

15 May 2004
1-229th reflags as 3-3 ATK
with AH-64D at Hunter
Army Airfield, GA

19 Mar 1964
229th BN (ASLT)
Activated
Ft Benning, GA

22 Aug 1972
Inactivated Ft Hood, TX

6 Jan 1992
1-229th transfers to Ft
Bragg, NC and assigned to
18th Aviation Brigade

23 Jul 2010
4/3 ACR reflagged as 1-229 ARB in Ft Hood, TX

1 Aug 2011
1-229th moves to Ft Lewis, joins 16th CAB,
and assumes its rightful "Tigershark" callsign

229TH AV BN

21 Sep 1978
229th BN Activated and assigned to
101st Airborne Division in Ft Campbell, KY

(ABOVE) This is a graphic that was produced by the leadership of 1-10 ARB at FT Drum, NY in order to explain to the assigned troops why they were changing the name of their battalion from Tigershark back to Dragons which was the name used when 1-10 flew OH-58Ds beginning in 1996. It also graphically represents the unintended mayhem that is visited upon a unit's esprit de corps when the Army changes the names of units.

1-25 AVN Battalion and Task Force Patches

INTERESTING FACT *On 9/11 "light" divisions in the US Army like 25th Infantry, 10th Mountain and the 82nd Airborne Division fielded attack helicopter battalions that were equipped with the OH-58D Kiowa Warrior. This was mostly due to the greater ease of deployabilty of the OH-58D versus the larger AH-64. As the war moved into Iraq and continued in Afghanistan, the Army retired the OH-58D from the inventory, restructured army aviation and the light divisions eventually equipped all their attack helicopter battalions with AH-64 Apache aircraft. Looking throughout this book you will see where units (like 1-25 AVN) that were equipped with the OH-58D proudly displayed images of the aircraft on their patches.*

RIGHT: An OH-58D being flown by 1-25 AVN at Camp Taji, Iraq in 2004 (photo by Author)

As another example of the problems an historian has in tracking down a unit's history, here is unedited the official history of 1-25 Attack from the US Army Alaska website. This is not intended of a criticism per se but it is included so the reader can see for themselves the often convoluted and downright bizarre nature of unit name changes and assignment.

The 1st Battalion (Attack), 25th Aviation Regiment was first constituted on June 21, 1963, in the U.S. Army as Company A, 25th Aviation Battalion, an element of the 25th Infantry Division. On August 12, 1963, the unit was activated at Schofield Barracks, Hawaii. The 25th Aviation Battalion arrived at Cu Chi, Vietnam in March 16, 1966. Despite being transferred to Vietnam without equipment or personnel, Company A (Little Bears) was equipped and manned with UH-1 helicopters from the 175th Aviation Company coming from Fort Benning, Georgia.

The 175th Aviation Company was inactivated and re flagged as Company A, 25th Aviation Battalion and served as an assault helicopter company. The 25th Aviation Battalion served in 12 Vietnam campaigns and received two Valorous Unit Awards and two Meritorious Unit Commendations. On December 7, 1970, the Battalion left Vietnam for Schofield Barracks, Hawaii. The unit was inactivated on October 15, 1985 at Schofield Barracks. During this time, the 25th Infantry Division was reorganized as a Light Infantry Division. The unit was later reactivated on January 16, 1986 at Wheeler Air Force Base, Hawaii. On May 16, 1988, the unit was re designated Headquarters ad Headquarters Company, 1st Battalion, 25th Aviation, and remained assigned to the 25th Infantry Division with its organic elements concurrently constituted and activated.

From January 1995 to April 1996, 1st Battalion, 25th Aviation regiment served as the Aviation Task Force Headquarters for the 25th Infantry Division (Light) during Operation Uphold Democracy in its deployment to Haiti. On June 24, 1999, the Battalion was reorganized when the last AH-1 Cobra Attack helicopters were transferred to the U.S. Army Reserve and National Guard units. For the upcoming year, the Battalion started fielding the OH-58D Kiowa Warrior at Fort Hood, Texas. After completion of the Unit Fielding and Training Program in June 2000, the unit went back to Hawaii. From February 2002 through September 2002, Task Force 1-25th Aviation deployed to Bosnia and Herzegovina as part of Task Force Eagle, Stabilization Force (SFOR) 11, Operation Joint Forge. The Battalion conducted reconnaissance and security, anti-smuggling, and special operations. The unit deployed to the Kingdom of Thailand from April 2003 through June 2003, in support of Cobra Gold 2003.

In January 2004, the Battalion deployed to Iraq in support of Operation Iraqi Freedom.

The unit conducted around the clock combat operations in support of ground units from the 1st Cavalry Division. Through July 2004, the pilots from Lightning Attack flew more than 2,000 missions. While originally attached to the 1st Armored Division, the unit moved to Camp Cooke in March 2004. The Battalion continued to support the 1st Cavalry Division in maintaining a secure and stable environment in Baghdad. The unit inactivated on June 9, 2006 and its personnel re flagged as the 2nd Squadron, 6th Cavalry Regiment.

On April 16, 2013 in a ceremony at Fort Carson, Colorado, the 1st Battalion, 2nd Aviation Regiment re flagged to 1st Battalion, 25th Aviation Regiment. The re flagging saw the rebirth of the Battalion and solidified its relationship with the 25th Combat Aviation Brigade who they deployed with to Afghanistan in 2012.

On May 20, 2013, the Gunfighters of 1-25th Aviation welcomed two AH-64E Apache Guardians. The arrival of the two helicopters marks the beginning of a fielding process for the Battalion. The Battalion is the second unit in the U.S. Army to be fielding the new Apache Echo models.

1-82 AVN Battalion Patches

A Company 1-82 AVN "RED WOLVES"

INTERESTING FACT: *This design was based on information gained via the interception of Taliban radio communications in Afghanistan. It was determined that the AH-64 was called "MONSTER" by the Taliban and on radio intercepts they could be heard saying, "hide, the monster is coming." So, with this in mind the 1-82 made this design which features a "monster" and the word "MONSTER" in Arabic.*

B Company 1-82 AVN "WHITE WOLVES"

E Company 1-82 AVN "BLACK WOLVES"

1-101 Battalion and Task Force Patches

A Company 1-101 AVN "SPECTRES"

SPECTRES continued...

PALADANS continued...

D Company 1-101 AVN "DRAGON SLAYERS"

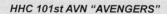

E Company 1-101st AVN "EXECUTIONERS"　　　　　　　　　　　　　　　**HHC 101st AVN "AVENGERS"**

2-101 AVN Battalion Patches

A Company 2-101 AVN "HIGHLANDERS"   **B Company 2-101 AVN "GREMLINS"**

C Company 2-101 AVN "GHOSTRIDERS"   **D Company 2-101 AVN "WARLOCKS"**   **HHC 2-101 AVN "PALERIDERS"**

3-101 AVN Battalion and Task Force Patches

A Company 3-101 AVN "KILLER SPADES"   **B Company 3-101 AVN "BLUE MAX"**

C Company 3-101 AVN "WIDOWMAKERS"

D Company 3-101 AVN "TIGER MAINTENANCE"   **F Company 3-101 AVN "LONEWOLVES"**

HHC 3-101 AVN "TERMINATORS"

2-159 AVN Battalion Patches

A Company 2-159 AVN "ASSASSINS" / "APOCALYPSE"

 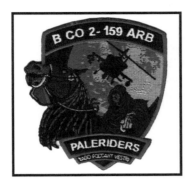   

3rd Battalion 159th Aviation Regiment "QUICKSTRIKE"

12th Combat Aviation Brigade, Illesheim Germany (AH-64A/D) OIF

3-159 AVN Battalion Patches

A Company 3-159 AVN "ACES WILD" / "PLAYBOYS" / "MISFITS"

1-227 AVN Battalion and Task Force Patches

C Company 1-227 AVN "VAMPIRES"

D Company 1-227 AVN "BONECRUSHERS"

E Company 1-227 AVN "DARK HORSE"

HHC 1-227 AVN "KNIGHTRIDERS/NIGHT RIDERS"

4-227 AVN Battalion and Task Force Patches

C Company 4-227 AVN "SNAKE EYES"

D Company 4-227 AVN "UNFORGIVEN" / "GUNRUNNERS"

E Company 4-227 AVN "EQUALIZERS"

HHC 4-227 AVN "BOUNTY HUNTERS"

INTERESTING FACT: *4-227 AVN and several other Attack Battalions (1-4 AVN, 3-3 AVN, 2-159 AVN, 3-159 AVN, 4-501 AVN and others) were organized and sent off to combat (some serving multiple deployments) where they performed their duties with distinction. Due to the reorganization and renaming of Army aviation units, 4-227 and many of its sister organizations disappeared from the active rolls. Their accomplishments and history are for the most part relegated to the memories of those that had served in them. The Army has a system that they use to determine what unit designation stays or goes, but it is unfortunate that the accomplishments of these units will for the most part eventually slip through the cracks and be forgotten unless those that know the stories take steps to make sure this history is preserved.*

4-227 AVN was re flagged as 7-17 CAV at Fort Hood, TX in October of 2015. What some might find interesting and illustrative of the process where units appeared and disappeared is that 4-227 was formed from elements of 1-501 AVN that were at Fort Hood in 2005 undergoing the transition from the AH-64A to the AH-64D Longbow.

1st Battalion 229th Aviation Regiment "CARD SHARKS" / "TIGERSHARKS"

18th Aviation BDE, FT Bragg, NC / 16th Combat Aviation BDE, FT Lewis, WA (AH-64 A/D) OEF, OIF, OIR

WINGED ASSAULT

1-229 AVN Battalion Patches

A Company 1-229 AVN "DEATH STALKERS" / "DEATH DEALERS" / "SERPENTS"

D Company 1-229 AVN "HAMMERHEADS" / "JOKERS" / "HAMMERHEADS"

E Company 1-229 AVN "MANIAC"

1-229th AVN Patches, note they were at that time in AVN Branch colors. It is rather obvious that someone in the chain of command was making an effort to make sure that company names would be different than other units using BLUE MAX etc.

3-229 AVN Battalion Patches

A Company 3-229 AVN "ACES ATTACK"

B Company 3-229 AVN "PREDATORS"

C Company 3-229 AVN "PROWLERS"

D Company 3-229 AVN "DELTA DOGS"

THE WARDING EYE

1-501 AVN Battalion and Task Force Patches

A Company 1-501 AVN "ASSASSINS"

B Company 1-501 AVN "DEATH DEALERS"

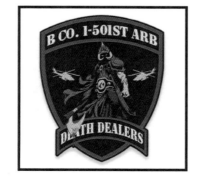

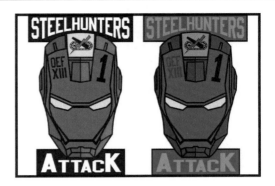

THE WARDING EYE

4-501 AVN Battalion Patches

A Company 4-501 AVN "PEACEMAKERS" | **B Company 4-501 AVN "PAQUEROS"** | **C Company 4-501 AVN "PALEHORSE"**

D Company 4-501 AVN "DESPERADOS" | **E Company 4-501 AVN "RENEGADES"** | **HHC 4-501 AVN "QUICKDRAW"**

AH-64 A's from 1-149th AVN, TX ARNG (2004 photo by author)

1-104 AVN Battalion Patches

A Company 1-104 AVN "REAPER" / "PREDATORS"　　　　　　　　　　B Company 1-104 AVN "OUTCAST"

C Company 1-104 AVN "REAPER"　　　D Company 1-104 AVN "DRAGON"　　　E Company 1-104 AVN "EASY RIDERS"

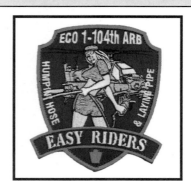

1st Battalion 130th Aviation Regiment "PANTHERS"

NC ARNG, Raleigh-Durham INTL Airport, Morrisville, NC (AH-64 A/D) OEF

1-130 AVN Battalion and Task Force Patches

    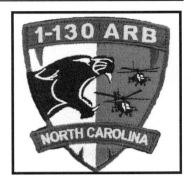

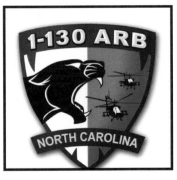   

A Company 1-130 AVN "RHINO"

B Company 1-130 AVN "KILLERS"

C Company 1-130 AVN "COMANCHE"

E Company 1-130 AVN "HAMMERHEADS"

1-135 AVN Battalion and Task Force Patches

A Company 1-135 AVN "DOGS of NIGHT"   **B Company 1-135 AVN "PHANTOMS"**

C Company 1-135 AVN "ROUGHRIDERS"   **D Company 1-135 AVN "HAMMER HEAD"**

1-149 AVN Baattalion and Task Force Patches

81

1-151 AVN Task Force Patches

A Company 1-151 AVN "NIGHTMARE"

B Company 1-151 AVN "MUSTANGS"

82

C Company 1-151 AVN "CHECKMATE"

HHC 1-151 AVN "SWAMP FOX"

L Company 1-151 AVN "DESPERADOS"

1-158th AVN Battalion Patch

A Company 1-158th AVN "ACES"	B Company 1-158th AVN "BULLDOGS"	C Company 1-158th AVN "CRUSADERS"

INTERESTING FACT: *The 1st Battalion 158th Aviation Regiment in Conroe, TX had been previously designated as the 7th Squadron of the 6th Cavalry Regiment. When the Army decided to restructure/ re-name its aviation units in 2008 the 7th Squadron 6th Cavalry Regiment was re-designated as the 1st Battalion 158th Aviation Regiment.. At the same time the unit turned in its AH-64 A aircraft and received new AH-64D Longbow Apaches.*

Unfortunately, the unit's history as an Attack Helicopter Battalion was relatively short lived. In 2016 when the Army once again realigned aviation assets, all Attack Helicopters Units were removed from the Reserves and most of the National Guard and 1-158th AVN was reformed as an Assault Helicopter Battalion and re-equipped with the UH-60 Black Hawk.

1-183 AVN Battalion Patches

B Company 1-183 AVN "FALCONS"

C Company 1-183 AVN "VULTURES"

D Company 1-183 AVN "ROADRUNNERS"

E Company 1-183 AVN "FIREBIRDS"   HHC 1-183 AVN "RAPTORS"

1-211 AVN Battalion and Task Force Patches

A Company 1-211 AVN "ASSISSINS" / "AVENGERS"

C Company 1-211 AVN "CORSAIRS"

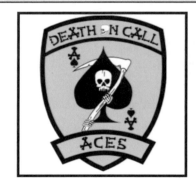

D Company 1-211 AVN "CANNIBAL PIRATE"

E Company 1-211 AVN "EXECUTIONERS"

HHC 1-211 AVN "HEADHUNTERS"

WINGED ASSAULT

8-229 AVN Battalion Patches

A Company 8-229 AVN "1st PURSUIT"   **B Company 8-229 AVN "2nd PURSUIT"**

B Company continued...   **C Company 8-229 AVN "HELL'S ANGELS"**

229th Aviation Regiment and the Flying Tigers (AVG)

Those with some knowledge of military and aviation history might be wondering about the 3rd and 8th Battalions of the 229th Aviation Regiment calling themselves "FLYING TIGERS". After all isn't the USAF's 23rd Wing the direct descendant of the 23rd Fighter Group which was formed during WWII from the remaining elements of the 1st American Volunteer Group (AVG) also known as the Flying Tigers?

The answer to this question is technically yes, but the story is, as many stories are, more complicated than that. During the late 1980's the US Army began to field the then new AH-64A Apache in large numbers. The fielding process included what was known as the Unit Fielding and Training Program (UFTP) which took place at Fort Hood, TX under the supervision of the Apache Training Brigade, which was later re designated as the 21st Cavalry Brigade. All units that were receiving the new Apaches underwent this training program. In 1988 elements of the unit that was to become 4-229th AVN formed at Fort Hood. Also in 1988, the 229th Aviation Regiment received permission from the surviving members of the American Volunteer Group (better known as the "Flying Tigers") to use their name and logo. After this all units within the 229th Aviation Regiment became proudly known as "Flying Tigers". At the conclusion of their training 4th Battalion deployed to and was stationed in Germany. In 1989 8th Battalion was formed as a part of the Army Reserve and at the conclusion was stationed at Fort Knox, KY. In 1991 1st and 3rd Battalions were formed and at the conclusion of training were stationed at Fort Bragg, NC.

At the end of Cold War, in 1994 2nd and 4th Battalions were inactivated. In 2004, 1st and 3rd Battalions were deactivated leaving 8th Battalion as the lone active 229th Aviation unit until 1-229th was reactivated using the aviation elements of 3rd ACR at Fort Hood, TX in 2010. 1-229th AVN subsequently moved to Joint Base Lewis-McCord, WA where they remain today. 8-229 AVN ceased operation of the AH-64 transitioning to the UH-60 Black Hawk in 2018.

It is interesting that the leadership of 229th Aviation in the 80's sought to align their unit's history with that of the AVG given the distinguished record of the 229th Aviation Battalion in Vietnam. The 229th Aviation Battalion served in Vietnam with the 1st Cavalry Division from 1965 until 1973. During that period the Battalion received 3 Presidential Unit Citations (The collective degree of valor (combat heroism) against an armed enemy by the unit nominated for the PUC is the same as that which would warrant award of the individual award of the Distinguished Service Cross) and a Valorous Unit Award with two of its members receiving the Medal of Honor for their actions in combat. That being said, when looking up the unit honors for 229th Aviation, it is worth noting that the Army's Center for Military History shows both 1st and 8th Battalion's name as "Flying Tigers".

The USAF's 23 Wing celebrates their connection to the WWII Flying Tigers (USAF photos)   *An AH-64 D from 1-229th AVN flying at FT Hood, TX in 2012 (photo by Author) and a Vietnam era patch for D CO 229th Aviation Battalion*

1-285 AVN Battalion Patch

A Company 1-285 AVN "ARCHERS"

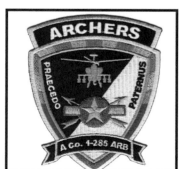

1-291 AVN Battalion and Task Force Patches

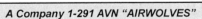

A Company 1-291 AVN "AIRWOLVES"

AH-64E firing rockets at FT Rucker, AL (photo by author)

1st Battalion 14th Aviation Regiment "TOMAHAWKS"

Hanchey AAF, Fort Rucker, AL (AH-64 D/E)

Various patches for 1-14 AVN and AH-64 Instructors

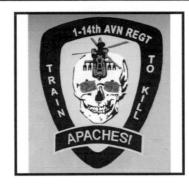

ACKNOWLEDGEMENTS

There is no way that this book could have ever been made without the help of a lot of other people. Below is a list of some of the many folks who helped in getting me images or actual patches to be included in this project. Unfortunately some of these folks are no longer with us. This hobby will be poorer in their absence but we are all richer for having known them. Everything good in this book is because of these fine folks.

THANK YOU!

Aeroemblem, Keith Alan, Apache Warrior Foundation, Aviator Gear, Emil Balusek (RIP), David Barber, Joe Belsha, Keith Benner, Bomber Patches, Steve Boras, Perry Bowden, Jack Brink, Steve Bull, Brian Carbone, Clint Chamberland, Jeff Crownover, Dan Cruz, Tim Dolifka (RIP), Kevin Dishner, Chris Dixon, Al Dupre, Rod Dwyer, Daniel Flores, Bill Fox, Carl Fox, Jake Gaston, Nate Graveman, Alan Hahn, Nick Hatchel, Glen Hees, Mark Hough, Aaron Joe, Eric Jurarez, Christopher Koth, Aaron Krupa, Billy L LeJeune, Jef Litvin, CW4 Matt Lourey (RIP), Angelica Maria, Jim McLean, Herbert McTacops, Samuel Mo, CV Nance, Ryan Nelson, Matthew Norbury, Steve Reynolds, Lea A. Rhinehart, Jason Richards, Angelo Rickert, Tom Rude, Alan Sanders, Steven Sandoval, Matt Silverman, Rocky Sudduth, Brian Serna, Dustin Smith, Keith Snyder, Jay Son, Shaun Steines, Tad Stuart, LTC Andy Thaggard, Shaun Thurman, Shon Thompson, US Company, Seth Vieux, Andy Wilson, Alan Woods

To submit corrections, make suggestions or inquires please contact the author at dngrpig@gmail.com

CPSIA information can be obtained
at www.ICGtesting.com
Printed in the USA
LVRC102323160122
708730LV00003B/30